TALKING ABOUT MENTAL HEALTH

AnneMarie McClain
and Lacey Hilliard

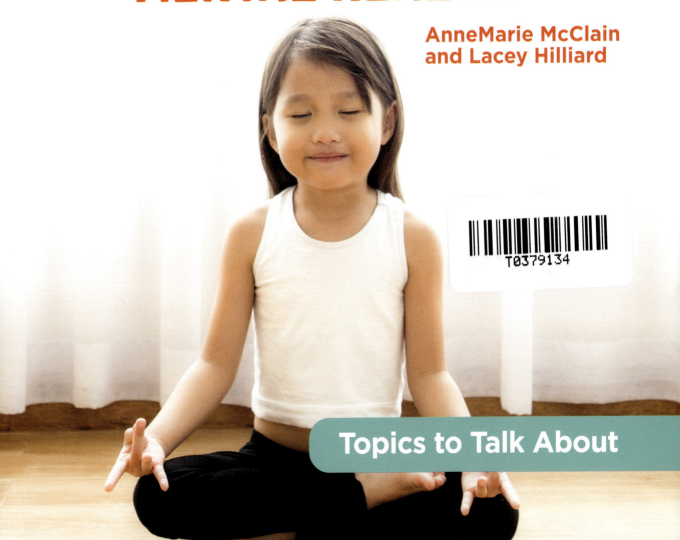

Topics to Talk About

Published in the United States of America by Cherry Lake Publishing Group
Ann Arbor, Michigan
www.cherrylakepublishing.com

Reading Adviser: Beth Walker Gambro, MS, Ed., Reading Consultant, Yorkville, IL
Book Designer: Jen Wahi

Photo Credits: Cover: © People Image Studio/Shutterstock; page 5: © fizkes/Shutterstock; page 6: © Monkey Business Images/Shutterstock; page 7: © Ground Picture/Shutterstock; page 8: LightField Studios/Shutterstock; page 10–11: © Prostock-studio/Shutterstock; page 12 (left): © Mary Long/Shutterstock; page 12 (right): © TinnaPong/Shutterstock; page 13: © AI More/Shutterstock; page 14: © fizkes/Shutterstock; page 15 (top): © Sunny studio/Shutterstock; page 15 (bottom left): © wavebreakmedia/Shutterstock; page 15 (bottom right): © Momentum studio/Shutterstock; page 16: © Ground Picture/Shutterstock; page 18: © BAZA Production/Shutterstock; page 19: © Mahsun YILDIZ/Shutterstock; page 20 (left): © stockers asia/Shutterstock; page 20 (right): © Nailia Schwarz/Shutterstock; page 21: © Keronn art/Shutterstock

Copyright © 2023 by Cherry Lake Publishing Group
All rights reserved. No part of this book may be reproduced or utilized in any form or by any means without written permission from the publisher.

Library of Congress Cataloging-in-Publication Data

Names: Hilliard, Lacey, author. | McClain, AnneMarie, author.
Title: Talking about mental health / written by Lacey Hilliard and AnneMarie McClain.
Description: Ann Arborr, Michigan : Cherry Lake Publishing Group, [2023] | Series: Topics to talk about | Includes bibliographical references and index. | Audience: Grades 2-3 | Summary: "How do we talk about mental health? This book breaks down the topic of mental health for young readers. Filled with engaging photos and captions, this series opens up opportunities for deeper thought and informed conversation. Guided exploration of topics in 21st Century Junior Library's signature style help readers to Look, Think, Ask Questions, Make Guesses, and Create as they go!"– Provided by publisher.
Identifiers: LCCN 2022039691 | ISBN 9781668920329 (paperback) | ISBN 9781668919309 (hardcover) | ISBN 9781668922989 (pdf) | ISBN 9781668921654 (ebook)
Subjects: LCSH: Mental health–Juvenile literature.
Classification: LCC RA790 .H55 2023 | DDC 362.2—dc23/eng/20220912
LC record available at https://lccn.loc.gov/2022039691

Cherry Lake Publishing would like to acknowledge the work of the Partnership for 21st Century Learning, a network of Battelle for Kids. Please visit http://www.battelleforkids.org/networks/p21 for more information.

Printed in the United States of America
Corporate Graphics

CONTENTS

Let's Talk About Mental Health   4

Kids and Mental Health   8

What's Most Important
to Remember?   21

Reflecting About Mental Health   21

    Glossary   22
    Learn More   23
    Index   24
    About the Authors   24

LET'S TALK ABOUT MENTAL HEALTH

Mental health is the health around your feelings and thinking.

Mental health is an important part of feeling good and strong. Everyone can work to be mentally healthy. Everyone deserves to have good mental health.

There are many things we can do to stay mentally healthy. Spending time with people you care about, and who care about you, can be one of them!

It can be easier for some people to keep their feelings and thinking healthy. It can be harder for others. This is okay. You can't tell someone's mental health by looking at them. People might need different things to help them think and feel positive.

You can't tell someone's mental health just by looking at them. Mental health happens inside a person.

Look!

Look at all these wonderful people. They are working and learning. Someone can only know how mentally healthy a person feels if they tell them.

Being mentally healthy does not mean feeling happy all the time. It's not possible for anyone to feel happy all the time! All feelings are okay to feel.

Mental health is a project to work on your whole life. Everyone can work on it. Think about being **physically healthy**. People eat healthy foods, exercise, and see a doctor when they need to.

7

Ask Questions!

What kinds of questions do you think experts ask people about their mental health? What would you ask a friend?

Now think about keeping mentally healthy. People talk about and take care of their feelings and thoughts. They may talk to a doctor or a counselor. Some people may take medicine.

Mental and physical health affect each other. How healthy your body feels can change how healthy your mind feels. How healthy your mind feels can change how healthy your body feels. People need to keep healthy in all the ways they can.

There are people who are expert mental health helpers. These can be doctors, nurses, therapists, and counselors. They can help with feelings and thinking. Family and friends can help, too.

KIDS AND MENTAL HEALTH

Everyone can work to be mentally healthy. Many kids and grown-ups work on their mental health every day! Even when their mental health doesn't feel perfect, they keep working at it. This is important because everyone should feel good.

It's important to notice when you feel other kinds of big feelings, like anger or worry. Those feelings are okay to feel. You can talk about them.

Make a Guess!

What might someone with great mental health be like? Would they get help if they need it? How would they handle tough days?

It can make you feel strong to work on your mental health. It might make you feel like you can handle anything that comes your way.

Having good mental health looks different for people. What works for one person might not work for another.

Choosing to eat colorful, healthy foods can help your mental health.

13

Kids can try a lot of things to feel good about their mental health. They can go outside or try something new. They can play with friends and spend time with family or pets. They can **exercise**, **meditate**, write in a **journal**, or play games. They can create something. They can talk about their feelings. They can help and take care of others. They can give or get a hug. They can talk to an expert helper to learn ways to help their mental health.

Playing outside can help kids be less anxious, more attentive, and happier.

15

Our emotions are there to tell us something. We can learn from our emotions.

WHAT'S MOST IMPORTANT TO REMEMBER?

Mental health is as important as other kinds of health, even if people don't talk about it as much. Making sure your feelings and thoughts feel healthy is important work.

Think!

Think of a time you felt disappointed. What did you do? Is there anything you'd like to try next time that you feel disappointed?

Everyone can do things to feel good about their mental health. There are things you can try and helpers you can talk to. Some of the things that help physical health can also help mental health, like exercise.

Things like stretching and exercising can help your mental health.

18

Getting out in the sun when you can may help you feel mentally healthy!

REFLECTING ABOUT MENTAL HEALTH

When was a time you felt a really fun or happy emotion? What was happening?

What can you do to feel good about your mental health? What would you like the grown-ups at your school to do to help kids feel good about their mental health?

When was a time you felt a really sad or angry emotion? What was happening?

What are some things you can do every day to improve your mental health?

Create!

Draw a picture of you trying something to help your mental health. How would you feel when you're doing it?

GLOSSARY

affect (uh-FEKT) change or influence something

exercise (EK-suhr-syz) moving the body to stay strong and healthy

expert (EK-spuhrt) someone who knows a great deal about a subject

journal (JUHR-nuhl) book or document in which people record their feelings and thoughts

meditate (MEH-duh-tayt) perform a mental exercise to relax, understand feelings, and be in the moment

mentally healthy (MEHN-tuh-lee HEL-thee) strong and healthy in your thoughts and feelings

physically healthy (FIH-zuh-kuh-lee HEL-thee) strong and healthy in the body

LEARN MORE

Book: *Naming and Managing Emotions* by Emily Rose
https://cherrylakepublishing.com/shop/show/52968

Video: Bridge the Gap Child Mental Health C.I.C. - "What is Mental Health? | Mental Health Explained for Children aged 5+ (2021, ~5:30) https://www.youtube.com/watch?v=uPh4-DU6MDU

Video: Anna Freud National Centre for Children and Families - "We All Have Mental Health" (2018, ~5 mins) https://www.youtube.com/watch?v=DxlDKZHW3-E

Video: Shandy Clinic - "Explained to Kids: Mental Health, Mind & Heart Wellness" (2019, ~1.5 mins) https://www.youtube.com/watch?v=eF7E8bvAyM8

INDEX

activities, 5, 14–15, 18
brains, 6, 9
counseling, 9, 14
doctor visits, 7, 9
exercise, 14, 15, 18
feelings, 4, 6–7, 9, 10, 14, 16, 17, 20, 21
happiness, 7, 15, 20
health care, 7–9

healthy activities, 5, 14–15
managing mental health, 4, 7, 9, 10–15, 17–18, 20–21
outdoor activities, 14, 15
physical health, 7, 9, 17, 18
social activities, 5, 14–15
talking about feelings, 9, 10, 14
therapy, 9, 14
thinking habits, 4, 6, 9, 10, 12, 14, 17

ABOUT THE AUTHORS

AnneMarie K. McClain is an educator, researcher, and parent. Her work is about how kids and families can feel good about who they are. She especially loves finding ways to help kids and families feel seen in TV and books.

Lacey J. Hilliard is a college professor, researcher, and parent. Her work is in understanding how grown-ups talk to children about the world around them. She particularly likes hearing what kids have to say about things.